W9-ALN-691

THE IRISH FILE

Images from a Land of Grace

Jon Michael Riley

Introduction by Nuala O'Faolain

Thames & Hudson

I wish to dedicate this work first to Catherine,

my special *Anam Cara*,

without whose help, encouragement,

advice, and love

I could not have completed my work in Ireland;

secondly,

to my two beautiful artist daughters,

Gillian and Lauren.

P R E F A C E

My journey to Ireland began as a result of several seemingly unrelated events. I had been reading a particularly vibrant memoir that took place in the country, which repeatedly brought to mind my grandmother's stories of her life in Ireland in the late nineteenth century. My mother, the youngest daughter of this same grandmother, had recently died, signaling the end of that part of my Irish family. At the same time, I had become increasingly fatigued by the demands of my work as a commercial photographer. I decided to go to Ireland to find my grandmother's village and to make photographs freely. I also wanted to meet the people there, to read their poetry and listen to their history.

In my trips to Ireland to take photographs, which I made over a period of three years, I found a beautiful, serene, and sometimes stark land about which my education had remained oddly silent. At first I thought I would photograph just the landscape, as I hoped to find something meaningful there, but my subject matter quickly diversified as I discovered the depth of the country's history and the warmth of its people. I photographed ancient and sacred sites, as well as the small metaphors of daily life. I photographed the people I met and the places they lived.

Although they are frequently hidden from view, I was fascinated by the holy wells that can be found throughout the country. There are hundreds, if not thousands, of clear springs that have been part of daily life and ritual as far back as the arrival of St. Patrick in the fourth century. That the blessing water emanates from deep within the earth, available to any sojourner, was of great interest to me. There are also many *slanan*, or healing streams, flowing in the Irish landscape. Holy wells and healing streams struck me as truly ancient and Celtic in concept, having little to do with organized religion, but everything to do with the spirit of the land.

Each well serves a different purpose. Some contain blessing waters for eyes, others for back problems, still others for stomach ailments, headaches, and so on. Because my wife, Catherine, who traveled with me, has multiple sclerosis and was not able to accompany me on some of the more rigorous photographic excursions, I collected small bottles of healing and blessing water from the wells to take back to her.

Just three days before leaving Ireland on what would turn out to be my last trip, I happened upon a special holy well just south of Listowel in County Kerry. A short path led downhill to a metal pasture gate. On it were posted directions to St. Senan's Holy Well and a short printed prayer that struck me as sounding at once contemporary in sensibility and Celtic in origin. As I paused to read the sign about St. Senan, a fifth-century monk, I was distracted by a distinct, haunting melody in the air. At first I thought it must be coming from a nearby car radio, but there was no one about — I was alone. Perplexed, I proceeded through the gate and onto the path to the holy well, which led me across a bright green field. Once there, I found a Marian grotto carved into a tall rock formation overlooking the small pool of crystal clear water that had been a holy well since St. Senan's time.

I decided to take a bottle of this blessing water to Catherine, so I returned uphill to retrieve an empty soda bottle from the car. Near the gate, I again heard the strange melody. The tune had an odd pentatonic or modal air; I stopped to look around for clues to its origin and to listen to it. In my puzzlement, I bent down to reread the prayer on the small plaque:

Lead me to the well of stillness

Deep into my being of God

Down through my thoughts, feelings, concerns, desires

Deepen and broaden it within me,

Help me to let go and to loosen up my life awhile

For your prompting.

To seep in through its sides in time

And fill my heart with your desire to direct my life flow.

It was at that moment that I discovered the source of the music: a chill wind blew over the ends of the open pipes of the steel gate, transforming the gate into a huge muted flute, with the shorter vertical pipes playing alto and the long horizontal pipes, bass. The sound was lovely, haunting, and celestial all at once—an ethereal song that seemed to emanate from the damp air.

By stopping me in my tracks, this strange music made me realize that this short, stumbled-upon prayer was an allegory for my time in Ireland. In three years of work on this project, I had been led to many "wells of stillness," and the effort and concentration required to maintain my photography during this period "helped me to let go and loosen up my life awhile." Being in Ireland, standing by that gate with the wind blowing across the pasture, was like cool blessing water flowing up from a great underground river. That moment—in fact, my collective experience in this country—was a gift to me from the land and its people.

Reflecting on this story which, at the time, appeared to be just part of a long day reminds me that, as Sir John Pentland Mahaffy once said, "In Ireland the inevitable never happens and the unexpected constantly occurs."

—Jon Michael Riley

If you live, as I do, in a part of Ireland popular with tourists, you become hardened to the transactions involved in photography. Your own mild bay and headland stares at you, lurid, from the postcards on sale beside every till. You shrug, embarrassed, at the garish images you catch sight of in brochures that have lured visitors across the sea to confront the singularly evasive reality of Ireland. You see the holiday makers lined up, laughing, their hair blowing across their faces for the friend who shouts, "Say cheese!" Their well-being will be there in the holiday snap, but the place where they stood might be anywhere. At a scenic bend of the road near my cottage, there are as many pointing lenses, sometimes, as outside a celebrity premiere. A local man tethers his donkey there, and he fixes a pipe between the donkey's teeth, and—click-click!—the tourists photograph the pipe-smoking Irish donkey. What else can they do with it?

And then, this. This American child of Ireland gives us these photographs.

Jon Michael Riley talks of thanking the land of Ireland and the people of Ireland for the gift of grace that came upon him when he was with us, making this record. But how to thank him for the gifts he has showered on us in return? Here is Ireland fully escaped from literary or historical text—pounced on by a lover who has had the patience to wait for it to reveal its secret, visionary self. These are the private beauties of an apparently plain and muted landscape, displayed for him, the lover, because he has stalked the angle, the light, the moment, when the beloved could be shown to best advantage.

His sympathy for the Ireland he both invents and records is all-embracing. Over and over, the drama within a photograph is the movement towards each other of the animate and the animate, whose coexistence can then be seen as a joyous affirmation of the shared organic being of things. His white sheep shelter under a hawthorn tree that is exploding with white blossom. His barn dog on Valentia is framed by old roof slates, stone walls, crumbling plaster, a wooden window half gone to dust: wistful dog and abandoned building belong together on some third cusp that is neither alive nor lifeless. The gravestones at Graiguenamanagh are one with the neat modern house behind them, and the figures of an outdoor Crucifixion scene mediate the young trees behind and the long meadow grasses that wave in front. The great bulk of the ceremonial mound at Newgrange stamps its authority on a landscape no less made than itself by human toil in the service of human need. Yeats' chair all but talks to his window. At Powerscourt House the stalks of the water lilies on the artifical lake wittily mimic the confusion of baroque and neoclassical beyond them. In the vision of this photographer, past, present, and the moment of the taking of the photograph are one, and this is the Irishness in him, seeing how it is here. Because neither ancient nor modern is the truth here: the mixture is the truth.

Stone things and living beings cross boundaries in the perception of this artist and move towards the condition of the other. The human beings—workaday, undecorated, innocently frontal—are shown rooted without self-consciousness in their places, even when the place is a wide strand and a vast sky. They touch each other naturally, delicately. They lead the loving observer to see things other than themselves—duck eggs, the curve of a statue of the Blessed Virgin Mary, the hull of a rowboat on a quayside, a head of Elvis, a field of cattle, the muzzle of a horse.

It is not the people but the stones that impress the viewer as compact with feeling. Stone heaves up through every surface. The path out from the gate of Pearse's cottage leads to stone outcrops breaking through the illusion of soil. Stone and grass meld in the ruins of Fort Dunboy, stone and moss at Lough Gur. An enigmatically carved stone, a millennium old, defers to the vivid day-old nettle at the entrance to Loughcrew. Diaphanous light plays in a tree above light's opposite, stone, and somehow sunlight, tree, and ancient stone belong—both in the actuality of the photograph, and somewhere out there—beyond interpretation. And stones themselves, in dolmen, barrow and ritual circle, swell and yearn towards each other in these photographs. Their curves are the loneliest things in lonely landscapes. Such is the empathy with which Jon Michael Riley approaches these prehistoric stones that when they are carved, he makes the carvings seem the voice of the stones themselves, calling to us in a language whose meaning we do not know.

No one could feel for Ireland as sensitively as this photographer does who does not know about sorrow and loss. In his images of derelict things half gone back to the earth—a rusting gate, the dried-out paint of a door, the corner of a ruined house already embraced by ivy—Jon Michael Riley adds his note to the lament for Ireland's tragic history of emigration and depopulation. Yet it is not these but his celebratory photographs that are the most touching of all. It is like the loving encouragement of a father for a shy child, what Jon Michael Riley has found to praise in a landscape usually only praised for its melancholy. This is the first time that I have seen photographs that say, "Oh, Ireland! You are sumptuously beautiful!" The sheen of the bay in a Connemara landscape, the exquisite tresses of water splayed on rock at Powerscourt waterfall, the dynamic greenness of a tree in a field in Cavan in high summer—these are images where grace abounds.

And yet they are true to the simple materials of which they are made. Ireland has half-drowned in its time in blizzards and froths and waves of words, storms and hurricanes of words, but words can never be precise—words are hospitable to as many images as readers can bring to them. Jon Michael Riley's Ireland is unified by one man's discipline: It is an Ireland presented not with passion so much as passionate control, as if the photographer had subsumed his ego to the spirit of the place and given himself to the particulars of its reality as his way of saying that he loves it.

—Nuala O'Faolain

THE BREATHING STONES

Landscape is not just there. It was here long, long before we were even dreamed.
It was here without us. It watched us arrive.

—John O'Donohue, from *Anam Cara*: *A Book of Celtic Wisdom*

A R T I F A C T S   A N D   M E T A P H O R S

... With a stone on the cairn, with a word on the wind, with a
prayer in the flesh let me honour this country.

—Louis MacNeice, from "Western Landscape"

WALKING IN THIN PLACES

The whole landscape a manuscript
We had lost the skill to read,
A part of our past disinherited;
But fumbled, like a blind man,
Along the fingertips of instinct.

—John Montague, from "A Lost Tradition"

J O Y   A T   R A N D O M

Quick! We have but a second,

fill round the cup, while you may;

For Time, the churl, hath beckoned,

And we must away-away.

—Thomas Moore, from ''Quick! We Have but a Second''

DANCING WITH ANGELS

Come away, O human child!

To the waters and the wild

With a faery, hand in hand

For the world's more full of weeping than you can

understand.

—William Butler Yeats, from "The Stolen Child"

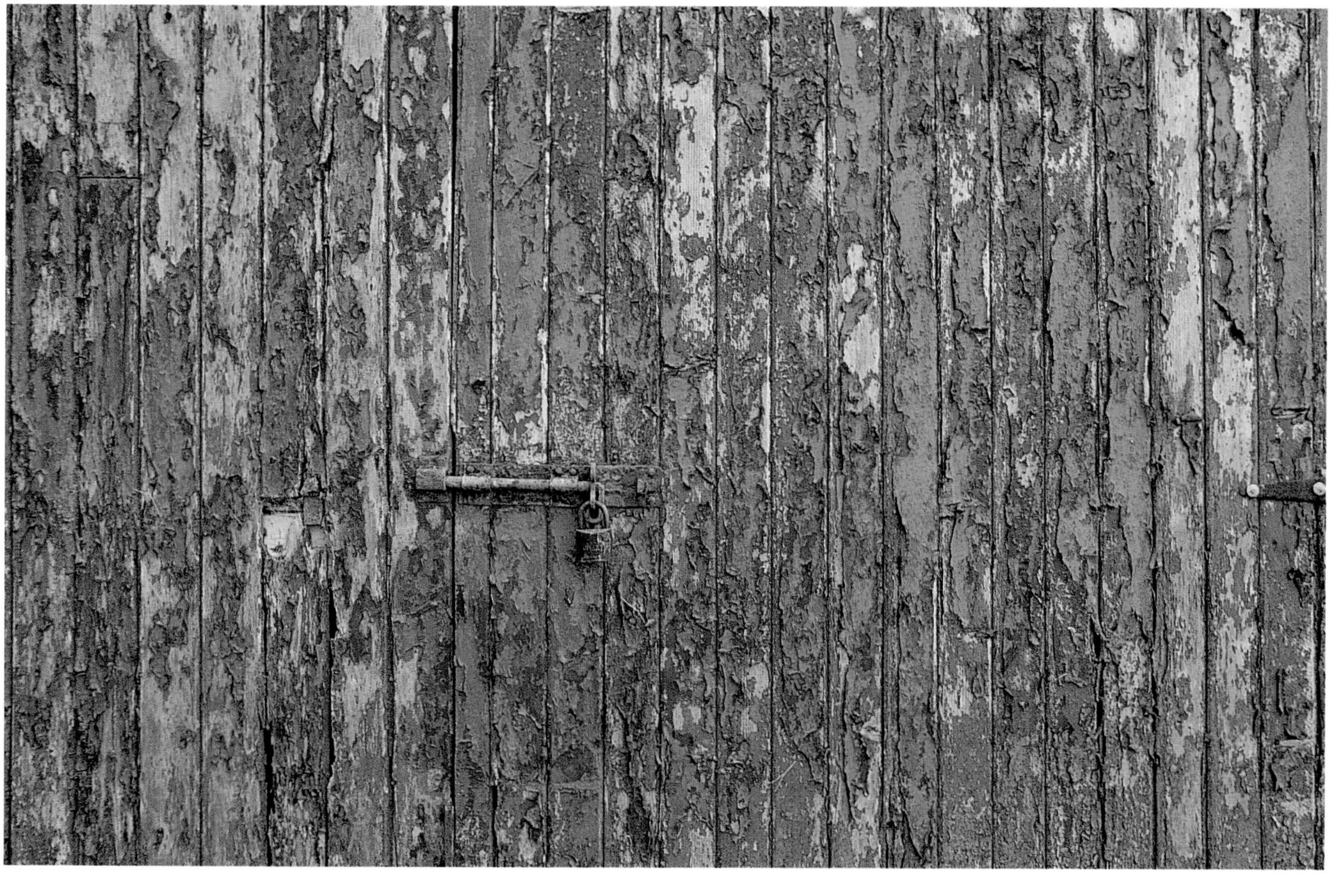

May the road rise with you,

May the wind be always at your back.

May the sunshine warm upon your face,

May the rain fall softly on your fields,

And till we meet again,

May God hold you in the hollow of his hand.

—Traditional Irish blessing

INDEX OF PHOTOGRAPHS

Inishnee, Connemara, 2000

Entrance, Newgrange, 2000

Barrow and mound, Loughcrew, County Meath, 2000

Standing stone, Lough Gur, County Limerick, 2000

Newgrange, County Meath, 2000

Poulnabrone wedge tomb, Burren, West Clare, 1999

Newgrange, 2000

Mound entrance, Loughcrew, 2000

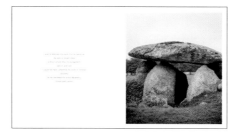

Haroldstown dolmen, County Carlow, 2000

Inscribed stones, Loughcrew, 2000

Boyne River and Newgrange, 2000
Great Stone Circle of Grange, Lough Gur, 2000

St. Patrick, Hill of Slane, County Meath, 2000

Emain Macha, County Armagh, 1998

Rock of Cashel, County Tipperary, 2000
Rock of Cashel, County Tipperary, 2000

Stone circle, Lough Gur, 2000

Rock of Cashel, County Tipperary, 2000

Standing stone near Clifden, Connemara, 2000

Apostles, Jerpoint Abbey, 2000
Dysert O'Dea, County Clare, 1999

St. Peter, Jerpoint Abbey, County Kilkenny, 2000

Glendalough, County Wicklow, 2000

Fort Dunboy, Castletownbere, West Cork, 1998

Holy Island, Gouganne Barra, West Cork, 2000

Gallarus Oratory, County Kerry, 1998

St. Finbarr's Cathedral, Cork City, 2000
Sheela-Na-Gig, Kilnaboy, West Clare, 1999

Jerpoint Abbey, 2000
Celtic crosses, Ahenny, County Tipperary, 2000

St. Fachtnan's Cathedral, Kilfenora, West Clare, 1999

St. Finbarr's Cathedral, Cork City, 2000
Corcomroe Abbey, Burren, 1999

Slea Head, Dingle, County Kerry, 1998
Clifden, Connemara, 2000

Kilkenny Castle, 2000

St. Finbarr's Cathedral, 2000

Holy Island, Gouganne Barra, 2000

Pearse's cottage, Ros Muc, Connemara, 2000

Powerscourt House, County Wicklow, 2000

Yeats' chair, Thoor Ballylee, County Kerry, 2000
Pearse's window, Ros Muc, Connemara, 2000

Garden of Remembrance, Dublin, 2000

Pearse's gate, Ros Muc, 2000

Powerscourt angel and Sugarloaf Mountain, 2000
Pikeman of 1798, New Ross, County Wexford, 2000

Wicklow Mountains, 2000

The ship *Jeanie Johnston*, Fenit, County Kerry, 2000

Hook Head Light, County Wexford, 2000

Beara Peninsula, West Cork, 1998

Hawthorne tree, Tara, 2000

Powerscourt Falls, County Wicklow, 2000

Healy Pass, Beara Peninsula, 1998

Connemara pony and foal, Inishnee, 2000

Valentia inlet, County Kerry, 1998

Borreen, Ballinlough, County Meath, 2000
Parnell's trees, Avondale Forest Park, 2000

Inishnee Island, Connemara, 2000
Turf, Ballaghisheen Pass, County Kerry, 2000

Connemara, 2000

Borreen, Tully Conor, Connemara, 2000

Clifden Castle, Clifden Bay, Connemara, 2000

Tommy Griffin, Knokerra, County Clare, 2000
May Fox, County Wicklow, 2000

County Cavan, 2000

Geraldine Ward, Inishnee, 2000
Seamus Doyle, 2000

The Blaskets from Dunquin, Dingle Peninsula, 1998

Boys with bicycles, Fenit, County Kerry, 2000
Tim and Mary Casey, Holy Cross, 2000

Mount Eagle, Dingle Peninsula, 1998

Lads of Kilkenny, 2000
Delma Carroll, Cragganouwen, 1998

Ruth and Richard, Glendalough, 2000

Liam Lynch, Dooniskey, County Cork, 2000
Dan Holland, Inchigeela, 2000

Johanna Prendergrast, County Kilkenny, 2000
Richard Connolly, Fenit, 2000

Howth Harbor, 2000

Billy Jevens, Cobh, 2000
Mary Crispie, Tralee, 2000

Slade, County Wexford, 2000
Cobh, 2000

Baily Lighthouse, Howth, 2000

Banna Strand, County Kerry, 2000

Portmagee, County Kerry, 1998

Wild goats, Stack's Mountains, 2000
Graiguenamanagh, 2000

Graiguenamanagh, County Kilkenny, 2000
Slade, County Wexford, 2000

Skerries, Fingal, 2000

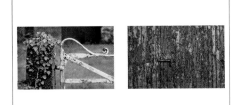

Inishnee, Connemara, 2000
Graiguenamanagh, 2000

Near Crossakeel, County Meath, 2000
Bannafoot, County Armagh, 1998

St. Senan's Holy Well, County Kerry, 2000

River Lee, Cork City, 2000

Kilkenny, 2000
Kilkenny, 2000

River Lee, Cork City, 2000

Hugh O'Neill, Dunmore East, 2000
Valentia Island, 1998

Clonmel, 2000

Glen of Aherlow, 2000

Roosk, Trafrask, Beara Peninsula, 1998

First published in the United Kingdom in 2002
by Thames & Hudson Ltd, 181A High Holborn, London WC1V 7QX

British Library Cataloguing-in-Publication Data
A catalogue record for this book is available from the British Library

ISBN 0500 542 554

Printed in Italy

A C K N O W L E D G M E N T S

I would like to thank the many people who allowed me special access to various places in Ireland or just helped me along the way: my editor, Elizabeth Sullivan, for her advice and council; Lynne Yeamans, for her wonderful book design; Nuala O'Faolain, for gracing this book with her beautiful prose; William Abranowicz, for his insight and advice; Noel Riley Fitch, for her encouragement; Ann Martin of the *Jeanie Johnston* Project; Tralee & Fenit, County Kerry; the public relations department of Newgrange National Historic Site and the National Monuments of Bru na Boinne, County Meath; the Reverend Dr. Michael Jackson, St. Finbarr's Cathedral in Cork City; Billy Jevens, captain of the *Spit Bank* in Cobh Harbor; Con O'Leary, Warder, St. Finbarr's Chapel, Gouganne Barra; Richard de Stackpoole, Stable Gallery, Roundstone; Eugene Markey, Cavan County Museum, Ballyjamesduff; Carey Conrad, Roosk, Trafrask, Beara Peninsula; Geraldine Ward, Inishnee, Connemara; Eamonn Butterly, Malahide, County Dublin; Margaret Teegan, Bishopstown, Cork City; Niall Williams and Christine Breen, Kilmihil, County Clare; and finally, Father John O'Donohue.